THE AUTHOR

Now retired after 45 years' service in the ministry, FREDERICK KELLER STAMM lives in Pennsylvania and devotes most of his time to writing and guest preaching.

A Congregational minister, Dr. Stamm has served pastorates in Pennsylvania, Ohio, New York, and Illinois. He is also well known as a radio speaker; his popular program, "Highlights of the Bible," was carried for nineteen summers over NBC under the auspices of the National Council of Churches.

Dr. Stamm has written a number of books. One of the most recent is *So You Want to Preach,* which Ralph W. Sockman called "a most helpful guide to those who are considering the pulpit as a career, a stirring stimulus to those who are starting their ministry, and a very practical aid to all who would preach better." Laymen will also appreciate the book for its warm and sympathetic picture of a minister's life and work.

I BELIEVE
IN MAN

I BELIEVE
IN MAN

Frederick Keller Stamm

ABINGDON PRESS

New York • *Nashville*

I BELIEVE IN MAN

Copyright © MCMLIX by Abingdon Press

Library of Congress Catalog Card Number: 59-7249

SET UP, PRINTED, AND BOUND BY THE
PARTHENON PRESS, AT NASHVILLE,
TENNESSEE, UNITED STATES OF AMERICA

CONTENTS

CHAPTER ONE

MAN IS A PERSON

I DO NOT KNOW WHO OR WHAT YOU ARE AS YOU SET OUT to read this book. You may be white, black, yellow, or brown, a man of prominence in some profession or trade or the lowliest of workers eking out an existence at some menial task. You may be the possessor of five talents or only one. Right at this point your social attainments, your economic status, or your intellectual ability make no difference.

I know only as I sit here talking with you that you are a man, a person who is different from anything else in the world. You are the only creature at the hand of God made in his likeness and image. You are not the equal of every other man in intellect, mechanical skill, personality, or perhaps even in spiritual capacity. Just as there are as many different thumbprints as there are people in the world, so your whole make-up is somewhat different from that of every other human being. But you are equal in this respect: you are endowed by God with life, liberty, and the pursuit of happiness. These were not given you by the country in which you were born. They were the gifts of God at your birth. It is the function of government, religion, and education to see that these are guaranteed to you inviolate. If they are not so guaranteed, then our whole structure of society goes to pieces. No matter who or what you are, you have an equal right with every other man to enjoy these endowments.

The realization of this ought to produce a just pride in the breast of every human being. God did not discriminate against us when we were created. If a person stands in the presence of others and feels his inferiority, he may still be sure that God did not forget to endow him with the capacity to love, to have faith and hope. When everything else goes, these are the qualities that abide. "Now abideth faith, hope, love, . . . and the greatest of these is love." Said Dostoevsky in *The Brothers Karamazov:*

Love every leaf, every ray of God's light. Love the animals, love the plants, love everything. If you love everything you will perceive the divine mystery in things. Once you perceive it you will begin to comprehend it every day. And you will come at last to love the whole world with an all-consuming love.

All this takes a lot of doing. It is not easy. But nothing in life is easy. The world is not an easy place in which to live. If God talked the way we do so frequently, I suppose he might say to each of us: "How nonchalantly you walk through life. I frequently become discouraged with you. I look for love and find hate. I see cowardice where there should be courage, revenge where there should be forgiveness and mercy, selfishness instead of unselfishness, misunderstanding taking the place of understanding. You are full of pride when you should cultivate humility. You stand in judgment upon your fellow men and regard yourself as holier than thou. You stand sometimes at the gate of heaven and sing like an angel and at other times at the mouth of hell and curse like a demon. You know the right thing to do in a given situation, but you don't do it. You think you are thinking about the problems of the world which effect the weal or woe of humanity, when in reality you are only rearranging your prejudices. You want other people to think well of you, but toward others you pour all the gall in your make-up into a slanderous tongue."

Our human nature is contradictory

A man may readily tell himself that he feels little or no responsibility for the world's guilt. He prefers to place the blame for the evils in the world upon the shoulders of an individual criminal or a group of criminals, while washing his hands of any inclination toward evil himself. Of course if we are one of those who believe in a personal devil with a pitchfork in his hands, having a horned head and cloven feet, we can easily put the responsibility on him and regard ourselves as victims of evil rather than its creator. God must stand amazed as he watches us. We applaud the progress made in medicine and surgery, in education and scientific discovery; we show our concern for the life and health of little children; yet at the same time we support the manufacture of the engines of destruction which threaten the extermination of the human race.

In short, we are all a bundle of contradictions and may well say with Maurice Maeterlinck: "I have never for one instant seen clearly within myself; how then would you have me judge the deeds of others?" Personally, I become discouraged with myself. I go to bed at night conscious of the fact that the day found me with sins of commission and sins of omission. I have done some things—perhaps no one but myself knows anything about them, and perhaps they have done no harm to anyone but to me—which I could very well have avoided doing. I have likewise known of some things I should have done but didn't do. I get up in the morning resolved to do nothing wrong that day or omit doing any good, only to find at the close of day that, although I may not have been remiss at the same places as yesterday, I still find other failures in my life.

I find myself with my full share of human nature. I know that though I have succeeded in putting some evils high on the shelf where they will not bother me again, I still have within myself the capacity to do them all over again. Whether the evil in my life was twenty years ago or only yesterday, it is still a symptom of my disposition. I wonder sometimes as I grow older whether I'll ever go to bed at night or get up in the morning with the full consciousness of having done all that is right, just, and merciful. This is not a morbid introspection. If it were, I would likely commit suicide. But I know that a man is a fool if he comes to the place where he can permanently neglect the condition of his own nature. I'll be sorry for myself and those around me if I ever reach that place, because then I should have come to the hypocrisy of the Pharisee who prayed, "God, I thank thee, that I am not as other men are." Just the same I'm discouraged with not being better than I am.

Do we really want to be like we are?

Man seems so many times to *want* to be what he is. I once heard a woman say, "It may be Christian to treat other races as equals, but I don't want to do it, and won't." Perhaps most of us do not state it so baldly, but our actions betray our attitudes. If folk move in beside us who are of another race or color, we move away and carry our prejudices with us. Churches, too, have the habit of following people into better neighborhoods where the race question will not disturb the conscience and where the preacher can sidestep the issue.

It is easy for us to whip up excuses for our race prejudice by assuming that exercising Christian grace means that "our daughter will marry a member of another race." It doesn't make any difference how far wrong we may be in our preconceived notions and ideas, we still remain as adamant as before. We like to surround ourselves with all our low ideas and prejudices. How small is our world! It is bound by family, the office, the home, the shopping center, and the school. It takes in a few friends, the people with whom we like to play cards or golf and go to the theater. We don't seem to care that there is a larger world —a world that is suffering because of our selfishness, a world full of people struggling for self-realization. They often get short shrift from us. We live by the dictum "It is their own fault." We watch the world bathed in tears and blood and think its problems can be solved without our concern.

A second area where we struggle is in the matter of world relations. I have heard all too many say, "I do not want to read about or to see pictures of suffering peoples in other lands. I see enough of it around me." Perhaps we are afraid that our sympathies will be aroused, that we will be persuaded to open our hearts and minds, that we will realize that we are not the only pebbles on the beach, no matter where or how we have been born.

I confess that I often despair of the world getting any better when I remember how many there are of us who think the Christian ethic of love and understanding is so impractical that we give it little consideration. Although man matures physically in comparatively few years, he seems to grow very slowly in his spiritual maturity. If he does not grow spiritually, all he can do about the evils of the world is to circumvent them, shut his eyes to them, or drive them out into some frontier wilderness like the Old Testament scapegoat who was supposed to carry the sins of the people on his back.

Again, I wonder how long we are going to remain massminded. I shall have more to say about the importance of the individual later, but just now permit me to tell you that so long as any human being feels his own puniness, he is on his way to state slavery, and without knowing it or wanting it he will become a nonentity. Most of us possess a good deal of common sense and reason, but we will never be able to bring them to bear upon the problems which afflict mankind so long as we look around to know what others are saying and doing, and so long as we quail before the big battalions of wealth, big business, and power politics. Shakespeare makes Isabella say in *Measure for Measure:*

O! it is excellent
To have a giant's strength, but it is tyrannous
To use it like a giant.

I am afraid we are surrounded by all too many "tyrannous giants" who fascinate us and overawe us all because we allow our individual personality to be submerged in mass organization.

Many of the commentators whose voices are the loudest make us believe that they are uttering public opinion. So we set about to applaud them and follow along like stupid sheep.

Since this is the case, it is small wonder that our individual best judgment often grows uncertain of itself and that our once blessed ideas go unexpressed. Then it is easy to hand the world's affairs over to those who deal in expediency and subterfuge and whose ethics fall far below our own moral and spiritual ideals. The result of all this is that the mass mind becomes the conscience of society, and whatever it says is right, and the individual is subject to autocratic rule and oligarchy.

Our deepest desire is to be creative persons

What I have been saying thus far seems to be the judgment which is passed upon myself and my fellow men by many people. I am aware, sometimes terribly aware, of the truth of these judgments. All we have to do to make us believe it is to look into our own inner selves and to note the human vice and folly about us. Still, I hope I shall give no impression that I despair of mankind. I can heartily subscribe to Shakespeare's Hamlet when he says:

What a piece of work is a man! How noble in reason! how infinite in faculty! in form, in moving, how express and admirable! in action how like an angel! in apprehension how like a god! the beauty of the world! the paragon of animals!

but I cannot conclude with him as he declares:

And yet, to me, what is this quintessence of dust? man delights not me; no, nor woman neither, though, by your smiling, you seem to say so.

If I should agree with this last, all the good purposes of my life would be defeated. All my work, all my preaching, would issue out into nothingness.

Soon after I went to the First Congregational Church in Chicago some years ago, I came across an old Armenian doctor. By the time I met him, he had fallen on bad times and was selling newspapers on the street corner. One day I climbed three long flights of stairs in a broken-down apartment building to see him. I found him half clothed and sitting on his bed, which was littered with newspapers and magazines. His hair was tousled, his beard shaggy, and neither he nor the room was very clean. I talked with him a long while and found that at one time he had been a rather successful physician. What had brought him to his present state of affairs I did not know.

A few weeks later a telephone call from a neighbor told me that the old doctor had suddenly died. When I saw him in his coffin at the funeral parlor, I was amazed at the transformation. With his hair cut and his beard neatly trimmed, I could see he had a high forehead, a patrician nose, full lips, and a square-cut jaw. As I looked at him, I said to myself, "I never saw this man before," and as I came from the funeral, I asked myself, "Why had I not looked through this man's exterior to what he really was? Or why had he covered up what once must have been a striking appearance?"

I do not know the reason. A dozen things may have accounted for it, just as a dozen things may account for the fact that we so frequently appear to the world as something other than what we really are or can be. Man is a person of quality, but he often does not allow himself to be seen. His speech, his actions, his general attitude toward life have made him something other than what he wants to be. In fact, according to what he says, he has been this way so long that it is impossible to be otherwise, and he says, "I am what I am, and I can't be something else."

If that is the final verdict that man passes on himself, it is little wonder that the world can expect nothing from him in the way of a creative contribution toward his own improvement or that of the world around him. People recognize a certain man because of the clothing he wears, the kind of complexion he has, his property, his rank, and his outward life. But they do not know him. The thoughts of his innermost being, his proper humanity, have hardly dawned upon them. Worst of all, he does not know his own *self*. He does not know that he is a microcosm, a little world, a reflection of the larger world in miniature. If he is ever to come to that place, he will have to assert the dignity of his own humanity.

The dignity of being a person

Human dignity means three things:

First of all it means that there is a spiritual principle within every man. Sometimes it is called reason, sometimes conscience. It is the thing that lifts him out of his local environment, rescues him from what is transient and temporary, makes him see and follow the truth of things and the everlasting right. It makes him realize that while he is living in an imperfect world which he will never be able to set entirely straight even in a long lifetime, there is, nevertheless, a right which stands in perpetual opposition to human selfishness and which he can do no other than follow.

It tells him in no uncertain terms that his neighbor is as precious as himself, other men's rights as sacred as his own; it tells him that his mind ought to be free to receive a truth no matter how it hurts his pride and to do justly, love mercy, and walk humbly before God, however it may conflict with his own individual interest. It is the thing that calls him to rejoice in whatever is beautiful, good, happy, holy, and in every individual in whom these attributes may be found.

If you could read Hebrew and would open the Hebrew Bible at the first verse of the first chapter of Genesis, you would come upon the word *b'reshith,* "In the beginning." "It is for the sake of making a beginning," says Martin Buber, the noted Jewish scholar, "that the world was created, for the sake of the human beginning-ever-anew." God made man good at the beginning and created him with the possibility of ever-renewing his goodness. He was made but little lower than God. It is this that lights up the divinity in every man. He will never know what he is entirely, but he can keep in his mind this principle of the celestial grandeur of his own soul.

Belief in one's own dignity will give one a second view of oneself. *Man is a free being.* He can act from the God-given instincts in his own soul and come to whatever destiny he chooses. He can realize that he is of the earth, earthy, but more strongly connected with God, and has the power to render or withhold the service due to his Creator. He is surrounded with a thousand warring forces; he must battle with the physical elements which give him pleasure at one time and pain at another. He sees dangers along life's pathway in the form of temptations, which if yielded to, can wreck his life; yet he can be endowed by God with power to contend with the temptations and to battle with the evil forces which threaten to overwhelm him.

Even if we are conscious of this power, however, we will not be freed from baffling questions such as: How can the world, as it is, be justified? How, if the world is what we see it is, can God be just? How, if God be just, can he be the creator of this kind of world? How often we have asked these questions! I doubt if even the godliest of men will ever cease asking them. But they can be resolved in the light of belief in God, who is not a contradiction between good and evil but who is wholly good and who wants nothing but good for his children.

Later I shall say more about a third element which dignifies man, but here let me name it as the *importance of the individual*. "How much then," asked Jesus, "is a man of more value than a sheep?" He is of infinite value, not

17

merely as a member of the community or as a contributor to the common good but on his own account. He is not a machine but a man. A machine is good only as it is a means to some end. Not so a man. He is not a means but an end, existing for the unfolding of his nature, for his virtue, and for his happiness.

In the play of some years ago *Seventh Heaven,* Chico, the sewer man, says to his companion, Rat, "Always look up, never look down. I always look up, I never look down. I am a very remarkable fellow." God made every man to be a "remarkable fellow" in his own right. True, he works for others but not servilely, not with a downcast spirit; he works for others with self-regard, from the principle of justice and benevolence. He is free and intelligent, and thus his character moves on to some degree of perfection.

It is for his own indestructible soul that he feels his dignity, not because of his birth, his success, his wealth, or for outward show. I am not a rhapsodist, nor am I just uttering words, but from a deep conviction born out of the very nature of God toward all peoples, I say that every man may well regard himself with as much respect as does the proudest monarch who rests upon outward rank.

Above all, we are religious persons

What has been said so far adds up to this: Man is a person, not an animal. And as a person, man has religious instincts. These may be covered over or badly atrophied because of disuse. But man has them. He may be terribly confused by the fact that often when he has gone to men who regard themselves as spokesmen for religion and to whom has been entrusted the cure of souls, he has been told that the facts of faith have been stated in concrete historic creeds and that belief in them can effect a miraculous transformation in his life. When he comes to think about this, he does not understand them at all, and the result is that he throws religion out of the window altogether. Conflicts are set up in his personality, and he begins to act as though there is no God in whom to believe and no soul which needs enlargement and fulfillment.

Man may get on quite well in this state until he comes up against a situation which he can't handle by his own mind or his own strength. Whatever the crisis may be— sickness, death, prosperity, or adversity, family, business, or personal problems—he not only comes to a standstill but becomes totally disintegrated, a split personality with a certain character at one time and a completely different character at another time.

I see no other way out of this disintegrating process in man than for him to set about exploring his own soul. Unfortunately, the tendency in most of us is to put off all self-examination so long as all goes well. There are potentialities toward greatness of character in every one of us. Whether they will be used toward good or toward evil, toward construction or catastrophe, in our own lives and in the lives of our fellow men depends upon how well each of us sits down before himself in an effort to discover to what use he will put his potentialities in any life situation.

The spiritual transformation of mankind will not take place overnight no matter how good a person may be. It follows the slow tread of history and grows quietly like a grain of mustard seed and will not come to fruition in a single generation. But one thing does lie within the grasp of every man—he can have a change wrought within himself and can find opportunity to influence others in the circle of his acquaintanceships. He will not do it by preaching to them or by persuasive argument. But by an awareness of right thinking and right actions in his own life, unintentional influence will be exercised upon the minds and hearts of others. As the Man from Nazareth put it, "The kingdom of God cometh not with observation: Neither shall they say, Lo here! or, lo there! for, behold, the kingdom of God is within you."

CHAPTER TWO

MAN IS MORE IMPORTANT THAN HE THINKS

I WAS IN GERMANY DURING THE TIME ADOLPH HITLER WAS spending a term in jail in Munich. Among the professors in Berlin University with whom our party held seminars and the German Reichstag members who entertained us, none regarded Hitler as anything but an upstart whose little popularity would fade out and who would be heard of no more.

We all know the history of the rise and fall of this man. Suffice it to say that the one man above all others who thought he was of importance was Hitler himself. In the early pages of *Mein Kampf* he tells what he set out to do. To paraphrase his words, he said: "I did not know at first that I could have much influence. Then I discovered that when I sat down with a couple of people, they listened to what I had to say. Then a little larger group listened and again a still larger group. By and by I found I could sway a multitude. They listened and were willing to follow me."

Thus his power and his following grew. Born in obscurity, frustrated in not being admitted to Vienna University to study painting, angry because he thought the broken morale of the German people lost them the First World War, he eventually found himself sitting as the chancellor of Germany and resolving that Germany would avenge its defeat. All the world now knows the diabolical character of Hitler and the men who surrounded him. The history of Germany cannot be written in all the future centuries without giving a large place to this one man.

I was a young man when I first began hearing and reading of Mahatma Gandhi. An Oxford University graduate, a lawyer, and somewhat of a dude, he eventually was stimulated by the writings of the Russian Tolstoy, and the Massachusetts philosopher Thoreau. When this little man threw away his Oxford clothing, dressed himself in a loincloth, and said: "I believe it is possible for a *single individual* to defy the might of an unjust empire, to save his honor, his religion, his soul, and to lay the foundation for the empire's fall or regeneration," there was general merriment in British and Indian ruling circles. Even in America he was looked upon as a fool. In jail and out again, resisting by "peaceful protest" the unjust laws, he brought justice to India and demonstrated the political power of his religious faith. When he died at the hands of an assassin, all the world mourned and knew that it had lost a friend.

What we do every day is important

I could go on citing the case of one individual after the other, for we all know that history has always turned around personality. A single individual can make rivers of water turn to blood, and a single individual can turn the doomsday of a nation into noonday. But it is not a question as to whether you as a man and I as another man will ever rise to the place where our names will be recorded in the pages of history. It is rather a question as to what kind of history we will make in the little world in which we move. It is conceivable that I am writing to someone who will rise to great prominence, whose voice will be listened to by the world, whose ideas and personality will change the course of history. Perhaps it is a young man or woman in high school or college, whose mind is just beginning to unfold, who will rock the world on its hinges and set its course in a new direction.

For the vast majority of the two billion people who populate the earth, however, this will not be true. What will be much nearer to their experience may be expressed in the lines of Edna St. Vincent Millay:

And life goes on forever like the gnawing of a mouse—
And tomorrow and tomorrow and tomorrow and tomorrow
There's this little street and this little house.

It is on this little street, in this little house, doing this little job, where the lives of most men are lived.

But that is no evidence that you are unimportant. When John Wilkes Booth was shot as he rushed from the burning barn where he was hiding after assassinating Abraham Lincoln, he held up his hands as he lay on the ground and exclaimed, "Useless, useless!" It must have been a frustrating feeling to know that never again could he extend those hands in helpfulness, but perhaps no more frustrating than the feeling any individual can have that he is of little or no use in the world.

Up the road a short distance from my home in the country is a little German shoemaker. When he hands my repaired shoes to me, he rubs his hand lovingly over them

23

and looks me in the face as much as to say, "Isn't that a good job?" And it is. No shoemaker ever repaired my shoes so well. He has plain human pride in his workmanship, the kind that goes along with the knowledge of a piece of work well done. In short, he is silently and stubbornly saying to me that no matter how many people there are in the world, he is still a person who counts.

The great importance of everyday work is best illustrated by the task of rearing children. The job of being a parent is important. In these days of juvenile delinquency (Was there ever a time when we had no problems of this kind?) we tend to think that religion, education, and the family make no impression on boys and girls and that the nation is going to pot because of this delinquent generation. We forget that there are eighteen million young people in the United States who never were, and are not now, delinquents. Most of the fathers and mothers of these young people are not wealthy. They occupy no high position in the religious, educational, or economic life of the country. They are plain, ordinary people with plenty of common sense and religious aptitudes, who realize the importance of being a parent.

A juvenile judge in Chicago once told me that not a single case of delinquency brought to his attention was the result of being born in a poor home. If you will talk to a hundred of your friends and acquaintances and learn something of their childhood days, you will discover that the large majority of them came from homes much like yours, where money was a scarce commodity. It is not money or lack of money that produces character. It is the loving and sympathetic understanding of children by parents who think child bearing and child rearing are important jobs.

We are important in God's plan for the world

Today, as often as not, we find people who are struggling against a sense of individual helplessness. Our world has grown so large, the problems so complex and overwhelming, so much is happening and so quickly, that we not only do not understand it, but we do not think that our little contribution is worth anything.

For one thing, our lives are being taken apart and put together again by some forces over which we do not seem to have any control. Our economic system has changed, burdensome taxes are laid upon the shoulders of both rich and poor, the public debt mounts, defense armaments of the most deadly nature are maintained, and the mechanization of life goes on to the point where a person seems less important than a machine. We hope the people who are the designers of the present age know what they are doing and that the forces about which we knew nothing a little while ago will not get out of hand. But for better or worse, we who have been accustomed to shape our own lives and make our own plans are being told what is going to happen to our families, our work, and our income. We hear it on the radio, see it on television, and read it in newspapers. Is it any wonder that a man begins to ask whether he has any significance or not?

Then too, a man is but one person. But when he is talked to by committees and correspondents and even by preachers, he is addressed as though he were a multitude: so many millions of people in the world, so many undernourished and handicapped people, so many millions in the armed forces of the nation. We are staggered by numbers. We know what a dollar is, but we do not know about a billion dollars. We know what one person is, but what do we know about a million people?

Our minds are crushed by the sheer manyness of things. Our sense of personal importance is lost in the midst of bigness, and there is hardly a piece of the world's work to be done that we can personally call our own. Does it really matter whether I am here or not? Is it important that I get my daily task done? If the country wants my son, I have nothing to say about it. It takes him and trains him, not in my way but in its way. And as to the major problems of the world—how to get peace and secure it, how to learn to live together in spite of our different ideologies—well, somebody may know what to do about it all, but I don't. The sheer complexity of the world gives us a sense of helplessness, until the helplessness almost becomes a religion. We say, "It used to be different. I counted for something. But now every man's hand is against every other man's hand. I'll succumb to the ideology around me."

One sure thing, this sense of helplessness cannot be cured by saying, "I'll stand up to what I believe. I'll conquer this fear by bravado." Resolutions of that sort do not help. The only way we can conquer it is by realizing that in spite of appearances to the contrary, it does matter, and matters eternally, what we as individuals do and say in any time of the world's history. If it doesn't matter, then nothing else matters, for to this end were we born and for this we came forth, that we might bear witness to the truth of God's universal and inexorable laws.

Our influence on others is important

There are a few reasons why a man is more important than he thinks. First of all, what we say and do is bound to catch fire in another man's mind and heart. States of mind are contagious. Practically all through my ministry the world has been sitting on the rim of a volcano. Fire and lava have been spurting from it which threaten not only to destroy one little city like Pompeii but to engulf the whole world. Two world wars have been fought, and bloody revolutions have brought agony and distress to multitudes of people. For more than a decade we have been engaged in a cold war. Not a newspaper issue has been printed during these years without some word about how wicked we think another nation is and how wicked other nations say we are.

As with many another person I sometimes listen to the radio, watch television, or read the newspaper with fear and trembling lest something has happened which will erupt into a deadly conflict that can wipe our little homes off the map, kill us, our wives, and our children, devastate our land and other lands, and leave the world a smoking hell.

In the midst of this kind of world, I declare that what you are, what I am, what the politician, the statesman, the preacher, the writer, the news commentator, the farmer, the mechanic, and the businessman say and do are terribly important. They won't go unheard or unnoticed in the little world where they move. No man lives his life in a vacuum. He is bound to have his influence for good or evil no matter where he lives or who he may be.

The sports editor of one of our metropolitan newspapers

published a letter for a baseball fan deploring the booing of the players from the stands and the chain reaction it may set up. He wrote:

Several of these groups of booers have children with them. The young boys join in the booing, since it seems to be the thing to do. On Saturdays, with knot hole gangs, these same kids no doubt start entire groups of boys to booing who wouldn't otherwise have thought of it. *Just think of the chorus to come when these youngsters grow up to be regular customers.*

And the editor commented, "Mental attitude is important."

We have a little boy in our home. He may someday live in a larger world than the one in which we live. What we give him in these formative years, he may give to the larger world in which he moves. What our motives are in his presence may become his motives; what we live into him, not by preaching or scolding but by a life that spells honesty, integrity, good will, may be the thing that he will live into the lives of others.

Among the thousands of letters I received during my many years on the radio, one stands out prominently in my memory. It came from a cowboy far out on the ranges. He wrote:

I am a cowboy down here on the border between Arizona and New Mexico. When Sunday morning comes, at the appointed time I tether my pony, sit on the ground, tune in my little battery radio, and listen to you. The first time I got you rather accidentally. Since then I listen because I want to.

I have lost knowledge of his whereabouts, but I have

not lost *him*. How many times I have thought of the importance of the words I spoke to him! Words! They can crush like the battle-ax of Richard or cut like the scimitar of Saladin; they can sting like a serpent or soothe like a mother's kiss; they can unveil the depths of hell or point out the heavenly heights of purity and peace; they can recall a Judas or reveal a Christ! I was only one voice among many to which he listened on his lonely vigil, and it was important that I spoke words which would have a chance to live in his soul and bear good fruit.

This is indeed a jittery age that can produce the jitters in us. It can arouse anger and fear. If we go about indulging them, it is possible that they will become the pattern for others about us. But if the words we use, the voice we employ, the manner in which we go about our daily task, reveal the steadiness, the calm, the poise, of our inner spirit, we will have more than an equal chance of transmitting these qualities to others. The point is, Do we realize how important all this is and how almost miraculously the atmosphere around us may be changed?

What I should like to get home to your hearts is the fact that all of us are important in the sphere which we occupy. As a person who is unlike any other person in the world, each of us represents something new, something unique and original, and something that never existed before. When Jesus walked the earth, he sometimes spoke to crowds but more often to individuals, and he had the happy faculty of taking a man out of himself, setting him down in the midst of his environment, and saying to him: "You have something to do. You are not a man apart from society, and you cannot live to yourself and for yourself.

29

You have a relationship to people and things around you." He told them, too, that if they would follow him, they would be changed men. They would have a new way of looking at life and a new way of living it. They had a certain life to live, certain thoughts to think, and a certain disposition to exhibit—all for the purpose of changing their environment. They would spread a contagion. They would be the salt of the earth.

If we could fully catch this, we could no longer feel ourselves unimportant or too small to count. Our attention would be turned from ourselves, our own worries, and our own plans to a responsibility for the general morale, and we would discover that other states of mind are the result of our own state of mind.

Our ideals are important

Again, every man is an important man when he sets out to make his ideals come alive. If I could sit down with you and we could talk together face to face and I would ask you what are the basic principles of democracy, the chances are you would answer, "Justice, equality, integrity, and common decency," or some such. These qualities came out of the very heart of God and worked themselves into the souls of men of thought and action. If I should ask you the basic principles of religion, the chances are you would answer, "Thou shalt love the Lord thy God . . . and thy neighbor as thyself." These words, too, were born out of the heart of God and found their expression in great and good men, and in the teaching and life of Jesus of Nazareth.

The fact is, however, that these words remain mere

ideals; they do not come alive in us. They have been float-
ing around in space rather than finding expression in individual lives. If the world is to understand justice, we
must be just. If liberty, equality, and integrity are to be
found in the world, it will be because we are liberty loving. We grant equality to all men, and our neighbors find
us to be men of truth and integrity. If love to God and
man is to be realized, it will be only when we base our lives
on these two religious principles. When the author of
John's Gospel wrote the prologue, he said, "In the beginning was the Word." Indeed, it had a beginning: it was
a dream, a plan for the world. But you can't stop there. It
goes on to say, "The Word was made flesh and dwelt
among us, and we beheld his glory." This is the history of
any ideal. It must become flesh, heard in a human voice
and lived out in men of dedication and human constancy.
It is only thus that it dwells in history and men can see it.
"Ideas" as someone has said, "have hands and feet," and
hands and feet must belong to a person whose mind is
animated.

When I visit the city of Washington, D. C., I do so with
increasing amazement at the guiding principles of our national life which are carved in wood and stone. I stand at
one end of the lagoon and read again the words of Lincoln
in the Second Inaugural Address: "With malice toward
none; with charity for all." Then I move to the other end
of the lagoon and read the words on Jefferson's memorial:
"Let Americans look into their hearts for the true source
of their political greatness, their uniqueness, and build
on what they find." Then I say to myself, "These are the
things which every man, little or big, known or unknown,

prominent or obscure, can have." My being swells with pride, not because we are better than any other nation but because these are what we can contribute to the world's moral and spiritual health.

Awhile later my heart sinks, for I am made terribly aware that in my own life these ideals are little more than reading matter. They are carved in wood and stone, burned into stained-glass windows in buildings, even in churches, but they do not become alive in the breasts of us who make up the nation. When I move out of my fanciful dreams and stand in the actuality of the present, I am amazed and frightened at the manner in which we discard charity and love, how we fail to look into our hearts for the true source of our political greatness, how we worship bigness, and how we quake in our boots lest we are not as materially powerful as Russia.

When I was a boy, my father and mother did not grow angry at the family in the village that had a larger home than we had. They did not tell me to be jealous of the neighbor boy who had a pony and a cart while I had none. They did not tell me to throw mud on the dress of the youngster who wore better clothing than I did on Sunday. They did not say to me, "We'll show them that we can have the things they have and wear better clothing than they." When I grew older and went to college, I had not learned to be bitter because there were other students who could enjoy more social life than I, whose fathers could afford to pay all college expenses while I had to work for much of mine. I had learned something deeper than that. I had learned that life does not consist in the abundance of things that man possesses, that life is not what a man *has* but what he *is*.

I believe there are families everywhere, even though they are economically secure, who live by that same principle and who teach it to their children. If I didn't believe that, I don't think I would go anywhere to preach next Sunday, and I'm sure I would not waste my time writing this book. People are just as good or better than my father and mother. They believe that a young man's successful career does not depend on what he *has* but on what he *is*. They believe that a son must be himself, not another. They believe that love is better than hate, good better than evil, honesty better than dishonesty, and integrity better than falsehood. If the large majority of fathers and mothers had not believed this within the bosom of their own families, we would be a nation of cutthroats and thieves, and no place would be safe for anyone. A poor boy would have no chance in life, education would be for the elite, and positions in the business world would be reserved for young men of wealth. We would be a nation of barons and serfs.

Yes, we are much concerned about our children. We want them to be law-abiding citizens. We have a sense of the imperishable values in life. But when it comes to putting our ideals to work in the *larger* areas of life, we think they are impractical. We showed ourselves poor in spiritual quality when Russia launched its first Sputnik. We were jittery lest the world would soon be blown to pieces, so we had to have bigger and better Sputniks. When we hear that Russia is strong agriculturally, industrially, and educationally, we must be stronger. We rest our case with material advantage. Spiritual quality is what we want to give our children in order to meet successfully the problems of their individual lives. But we find it difficult to conceive that we are what we are, not because we have been strong in nuclear weapons but because out of our hearts we have let our honesty, integrity, and helpfulness shine into all the world.

The cause we serve is important

A third reason why we dare call ourselves important men is because we can be walking, talking examples of what freedom in democracy and religion can produce. How convincing are we, not by any arguments we may advance but in all our habits and actions, that what we have is worth all its cost?

We pick up newspapers and read of countries far away whose people are oppressed, whose lands have been confiscated, and whose struggles against tyranny have resulted in imprisonment and death. We talk about it in groups, in our homes, with our business associates, and with our neighbors, and we wish that freedom would be so valuable in the eyes of all downtrodden people that they would be willing to risk their necks for it. Then they look at us and our democracies. They expect to find men of large mental and spiritual stature who have been shaped by freedom. Do they find in us not merely an official difference but a marked difference between men of a democracy and a dictatorship? Do we treat one another as equals? Do we take an interest in the common welfare, in our brothers? Do we carry on our economic and religious affairs in strict honesty? If there is no marked difference, then what is the value of having been born and reared in a free country?

Democracy is still an expanding idea. It was not set down here in our country more than three hundred years ago all perfectly made up. What good there is in democracy—and there is much—is the result of good thinking and noble actions on the part of good and noble men. Evils that were once here are no longer tolerated. Like Abraham of old, our forefathers went out into a land they knew not, but they went out in faith. They pitched their tents, built cities, cleared the land, founded schools and colleges and churches. Along with their material interests they did not forget to rear an altar to God. Not all they did was good. Some things were very bad. But men were reared in this environment, and the improvement of the environment has been due to men of honesty, integrity, and good will.

Democracy is still here, better in many respects than when our forefathers founded it and worse in other respects. But it is still here, and we are living in it. What it will be tomorrow depends upon us. For example, we have had freedom of speech. Men have tried to interfere with free speech and have been all too successful. Patriotism has assumed to be what some misguided zealots thought it should be—a blind acceptance of all the falsehoods and propaganda about other peoples, a submersion of anything that looked toward justice, truth, or understanding. Sentences in speeches and writings have been lifted out of context in order to prove the guilt of honest citizens. Many honest preachers and statesmen who have tried to fit their messages to the times and do it with an eye single to the glory of God, have been haled before tribunals where the guilt had already been assumed.

If we are men of principle and lovers of truth, we will

cry out against these injustices. We may be only one in our community, but if we look around, we will find others of like mind who are just waiting to hear an encouraging and truthful word from us. Phillips Brooks once preached a sermon on the text "The spirit of man is the candle of the Lord." How else will God's light shine into the darkness unless we and a host of others light our candles with the spirit of God? Robert Louis Stevenson wrote, "Behold, how many candles can be lit all around the world!"

We have had the chance, too, to practice free religion. With what searching humility and human dignity have we practiced it? We have had a chance to be decent and respectable toward others of another race and color. Yet the struggle for integration goes on. There is nothing in religion that teaches us to be cruel to anyone. Yet we have been cruel in assuming that God has set some to be masters and others slaves.

Perhaps we have not asked ourselves questions that are pointed enough; consequently we share no responsibility for their answer. I hope you and I do not belong to those with cynical notions about the irreconcilable selfishness of mankind. If I believed that, I couldn't preach and I couldn't write to you. My belief is that no one can ever make out a case for himself on the basis of selfishness. I believe that good men are made when they discover that they can serve themselves best when they serve a cause larger than themselves. It is this belief that I hope will make you feel as you read this book that you are more important than you think.

CHAPTER THREE

MAN CAN HAVE A FIRSTHAND ACQUAINTANCE WITH GOD

OVER THE YEARS IT HAS BEEN MY PRIVILEGE TO KEEP IN touch with the thinking of young people other than those of my own family and my own church by teaching "The Life of Jesus Christ" to several groups of high school students at a youth conference. One summer as I went to the same conference for the third successive year, the same old concern troubled me—how to make Jesus a reality in the lives of these youngsters.

How to give them a bit more knowledge of the man who walked the streets of cities and the lanes of Palestine did not greatly concern me. But how to make that life so fascinating as to produce a desire to be like him is another question, for I think I need not tell you that religion is one thing and the study of religion is another.

Not all the people to whom Jesus spoke caught his spirit and felt his life flowing into theirs, and one could hardly expect that fifty or more young people would find any appreciable difference in their lives after a week of religious instruction. But I hoped that here and there there might be *one*. Sure enough after I returned home last summer, a beautiful letter came from one young girl. She wrote: "I am the Negro girl who sat in the front seat, and

I want to tell you I absorbed your words for they really hit home. You touched me deeply, and I hope to grow up to be the kind of Christlike character you showed me to be."

I tell this little incident because it is my conviction that the study and discussion of religion is too often made to do duty for religion itself. Someone said long ago that the moment we begin the discussion of religion it is apt to leave us. But I could hope that when this chapter is ended and you begin to reflect on it, you can pick up a more vital religion and immerse yourself more completely in the silence of a divine faith. If you fail to do this, then religion will be only an intellectual exercise.

Despite the fact that there has been criticism leveled at the religious instruction in our churches, I believe that it has been done pretty well. Devoted and intelligent men and women have always been seeking saner and better methods of religious instruction. Then too, when I compare the facilities for religious instruction with what they were when I was a boy, I know that the religious development of the generations has been the deep concern of thousands of men and women everywhere. But even so, instruction in religion can produce little more than a ghost of religion. It is right here that man's outreach for religion gets bogged down. He wants the touch of God upon his life and soul, an experience that makes him know that his life is bound up in God, and what he gets so frequently in his quest is a discussion *about* God. We build theological seminaries where youth are instructed in religion and sent out to preach the Good News. We build beautiful sanctuaries where God may be worshiped in the beauty of holiness, and we equip our churches with up-to-date educational facilities. But still we are haunted by the fact that religion in the lives of so many of us is only a ghost of religion rather than what it really can become in the life of man.

What is religious experience?

Many years ago William James wrote his classic work on the *Varieties of Religious Experience.* It was written to send people back to the study of religion, and it accomplished its purpose. More books were written on similar subjects which were designed to make the study of religion more scientific. They no doubt started any number of people in pursuit of a more intelligent knowledge of religion, but it may well be doubted if they have done much to impart a religious experience to the man who had none before or to deepen the religious experience of the man who already had it.

What it did do was to create the impression that religious experience is confined to a small group of saints, and that it could never happen to the large number of plain men and women. Personally, I have discovered that most of the people whose religious experiences have been described in books were abnormal in their make-up and not like myself at all. These people were abnormal in the qualities they possessed and in the virtues they lacked. We could by no means deny that their testimony is true, but if most of the men and women in the world are made of the same stuff as I am, then this kind of testimony tends to set them apart from the rank and file of ordinary people.

The result of all this has been unfortunate. The experiences of certain individuals too often leave the plain man, who probably never had such an experience himself or is unable to recognize it if he has, mystified and wondering if he is religious at all.

I confess that I sometimes have this feeling myself when I read books about strange religious experiences or when I hear spiritual practitioners of a certain type who go about the country telling of the rapture and vision which they and other special souls have had. Visions have never been mine, and I have a suspicion that they will never be. I do not question their validity, and I am perfectly willing to believe that these men have realized their quest for reality. But as for me, I am denied such experiences. I have a conviction that any number of you share my feeling. Are we spiritually dead? Are we ignorant of what a religious experience is? Can't we know God in his fullness? Has God excluded us from his presence? Or have we committed the unpardonable sin against the Holy Ghost? I read of a man who felt so. Failing to respond to some evangelist in the way that was expected, he was told that he had committed the unforgivable sin. He took it to heart. He tried to discover what he had done. It was now this, now that. Every other sin he could identify but not this one. After months of appalling misery he was sunk in despair and became a suicide.

Such things are not advertised. Like the old patent medicine shows, only the successes are announced. The failures are passed over in silence. But they can be found on the fringes of the present-day evangelistic crusades and in the wake of movements which promise a deep religious experience on condition that a certain technique be adopted and a certain phraseology used.

If the appeal to you for a religious experience has been made on grounds that make you conclude that you are not naturally religious and that you do not belong to the company of privileged souls, I wish that something more might be said. I would say to you that religion is not a delusion, that the exceptional souls are no wiser than you with your own ways, and that you need not stand embittered against religion and the promoters of religion.

How do we recognize religious experience?

First of all we should realize that there can be a genuine religious experience in those happenings which, at the time, did not seem to be religious at all. Perhaps we have had a very unhappy experience in life, something which seems to remove us from God as far as we can ever be, some sense of frustration, some failure in our outreach for God. "Come," says the psalmist, "behold the works of the Lord, what desolations he hath made in the earth." What desolate hearts we have! What hopes deferred! What disappointments! I once knew a man of seventy whose pension was denied him because of a technicality. His wife took a small job. Soon sickness overtook her, and she died. His small savings were exhausted, and he took refuge in drink. He was a beggar on the streets asking alms from passers-by. He was rescued by kind friends, placed in a good home, his confidence returned, and God became more strongly than ever a reality. It often happens that when it seems we are furthest from God, these are the moments when we have our experience of God that is almost too glorious for description.

The difficulty with religious experience is to recognize it when it comes to us. God is always coming our way. We are like Jacob, who slept on the mountaintop all night and did not know that he was in the house of God at the gate of heaven until morning.

Somehow mankind is in the habit of thinking that a religious experience is yet to come, when the fact is, it is always present in the deepest silences of our life. If we keep our minds only on the experiences of the great saints and forget that we too have hearts fit for the dwelling place of God, we are in danger of missing the normal currents of God which flow about us all the time.

Again, a man can have an experience of God when he realizes that God does not reserve his favor for rare and exceptional souls. The ordinary man can't move very far in life without discovering that he is upheld, supported and animated, directed and moved forward to a better life by a Power in which he lives and moves and has his being. Not merely some special experience but daily and momentary experiences which ordinary people feel and recognize when their attention is called to them are experiences of God. Years ago I came out of a little country schoolhouse with a man on a brilliantly starry night. He looked up and said, "Who can doubt that there is a God? Not only because he set the stars and the planets in their course in the heavens but because he made *me* and set bounds to my habitation." It wasn't a mystic experience of God; he saw no face and heard no voice. But it was the kind of experience well within the reach of the average wayfaring man.

What I am trying to say is that all human experience, when rightly understood, is a spiritual experience. If I walk down the road with a heart full of love for my neighbor and our conversation lifts us both out of ourselves, it is a spiritual experience for both of us. If I beautify my lawn and make a stony place in my garden to blossom as the rose, God is in the work. If I make the little place called the world in which I live a better place for men and women and little children to live in, it is a spiritual experience which sends me to bed at night feeling that I am a co-laborer together with God. We should never completely separate religious experience from experience in general, for even in the most familiar experience we can feel the touch of the Spirit of God.

Thomas Carlyle once fell into conversation with the new minister who had been appointed to his parish. Said Carlyle, "What this parish needs before anything else is a preacher who knows God otherwise than by hearsay." When Ralph Waldo Emerson was giving advice in his divinity school address, he said that the one thing needful above all others was "a firsthand acquaintance with Deity." If we would put these two statements together and make them read, "A firsthand acquaintance with Deity is a knowledge of God otherwise than by hearsay," we would have something of vital importance for men and women everywhere. It would be wrong for me to tell you that this is the last word in religion, but we *can* call it the first in the sense that whatever higher forms the religious life may take, they all stem from this point.

Men have always searched for God

When spiritual hunger comes, a man can always go to the Bible and find the things that will satisfy his hunger. For it is in the Bible that we find natural religion, religion that is spontaneous, unstudied, and firsthand. There is no attempt to cover up or gloss over the faults of its heroes.

It is a picture book of the experiences that repeat themselves in every generation. There isn't a single human experience today which cannot be paralleled in the Bible. And no matter how sordid some of the narratives may be, there is always a consciousness of the divine Presence, guiding and sustaining weak and faulty men. They could never get away from God.

Our day our surroundings, our way of life, are quite different from those of the biblical characters. But human nature, being what it is, has the same heart, the same conscience, the same hopes and desires, the same needs, in one age as in another. Examining ourselves we find that in many respects we are not unlike people of a far-off age, and the same ways of finding God are open to us as were open to them.

An old story, older than any living religion, goes back to the very morning of time when men thought there were many gods, not one. The gods met together, and in the midst of their deliberations man entered and claimed that he was akin to the gods. The gods were silent when they heard this presumptuous upstart. But being just, they listened to the evidence put forth by man, and they were compelled to admit that his claim was true.

However, the gods were jealous and stole the divinity of man. They knew they had no right to have it and they met again to decide what to do with it. There was no place they could think of where it would be safe.

At last the oldest and the wisest of the gods said, "Give it to me; I know where to hide it." It was agreed, so his hand closed over the tiny, precious speck of god-fire—the secret of the restless soul of man.

When he opened his hand, it was gone. "All is well," he said. "I have hidden it in man himself, as that is the last place he will ever think to look for it. Our secret is safe." Nor would he tell where in man he had hid it.

Here is the great fact about man—an inner urge, an endless search for beauty, truth, goodness, and meaning in life. Man would not desire God were not God already with him. Nor would he ever feel denied, alone, forsaken, if God had never been near. It is God himself who moves men to seek God. In short, there could be no religion if the object of religion did not exist. Nor would any man ever go out in search of truth if truth were a mere fancy. If we could prove God by logic, it would be too easy. It would leave the soul undeveloped.

How we find God

There are ways, however, of finding God and having a firsthand acquaintance with him. In John Drinkwater's great play *Abraham Lincoln* the author depicts a scene in the White House just before the beginning of the Civil War. Secretary Seward had been somewhat in disagreement with President Lincoln, but when Lincoln pointed out the falsity of his position, he turned to Lincoln and said, "I'm sorry. I had not been thinking the matter through carefully enough."

In that historic incident we see one of the ways by which a man may find God—by acknowledging faults. Sometimes a strong man may find it humiliating to acknowledge an error. But it is at this very place that the courage of men breaks down. There is no healing power in such a hard faith in oneself. See how it works. Somewhere in our life there has been an act which has destroyed or imperiled some human relationship. We acted as though it did not matter. We have gone on deluding ourselves with the idea that the final achievement of our life will cover up and conceal the old wrong. Our false pride makes us unwilling to stoop to the difficult and humiliating process of undoing the harm that once was done. We would rather pretend that it never existed, and since it happened a long time ago, by now it does not matter. We keep the old uneasiness buried so that it does not disturb us. But if we do succeed in doing that, it is by so much damage to ourselves. We may be satisfied but never great. The great souls in the world are those who see their shameful action, their mean motives, self-indulgence, deceit, and cowardice. And when a man sets these up against a standard of right, it will always be true that his conscience will speak to him. By keeping a lively conscience one is bound to come upon God face to face; by stifling conscience until it becomes dead, God will be shut out.

We can know God also in action—in the things we do. In what wrong directions do we so often go seeking God! We ask for assurance. "Show us a sign," we say, just as men said to Jesus two thousand years ago. We look for the sign of God, some miracle that will be an indisputable evidence that God is. We hope to experience some strange feeling, something that will produce a "click," that will prove without question that we have come face to face with God. Some of us hope to prove God by some mechanical calculation. We want to prove God just as we prove that two times two are four, and that a straight line is the shortest distance between two points, or that oxygen and hydrogen produce water. A god that can thus be proved by the human mind isn't God.

Many people do not find God because they do not go where he would have them go. Too many of us stay within the limit of our own group, pandering to one another's vanities and bolstering up one another's prejudices. But we will never find God in that atmosphere, no matter how often we attend church or how much we delight in the preacher's utterances. Let us go out and do something for someone. Let us lose ourselves in a cause, travel up some dark stairway, mingle with the so-called publicans and sinners, see how the other half of the world lives, put ourselves under another person's burdens, look through our neighbor's window and see how the world and life look to him. If we don't come across God in some of these travels, then there is no God, and we will be justified in going our own way. But if we take the blinkers from our eyes, we will come upon God in his glory.

Then too, we can have a firsthand acquaintance with God when we put to constant exercise the best in ourselves. We've made a lot of this word "hypocrite," and we like to roll it under our tongue, especially when we see someone whose deeds belie his profession. During a trial of a man for murder, I noticed in the newspaper that every time his name was mentioned, the reporter brought in "and former church worker," as though his churchliness had something to do with the crime. Yes, we like to point the finger at the hypocrite. But how about those of us who are constantly trying to appear less good than we are? We put the worst in the show window. Many of us do that. We act as though we were ashamed of goodness—ashamed to face the world in an armor of righteousness—and in our denial we lose God. Down deep in every person's heart are good impulses, noble emotions, kind thoughts, and potential greatness. These qualities are not supposed to be kept "deep down"; they belong on the surface, not for the purpose of showing off to the world but because these are the motives by which we must live and act.

> To thine own self be true,
> And it must follow, as the night the day,
> Thou canst not then be false to any man.

We can find God, too, in noble lives. A man, lying on his deathbed, looked up at his wife and said, "In your face I have seen the eternal." Doubtless it is through others that most of us have come to have genuine faith in God. A good friend of mine died after a very brief illness in a Roman Catholic hospital. The sisters moving about and observing his last hours said, "We have never seen anyone like him." What he believed about the Bible or creeds or dogmas sank into the background, and all differences were obscured in the greatness of the person who had staked his belief in these great words, "Being justified by faith, we have peace with God through our Lord Jesus Christ."

Yes, we see God in the Godlike qualities of a great soul. One of the treasures in my library is an autographed copy of *The Labrador Doctor* by Sir Wilfred Grenfell. He came to our home one evening and later spoke in my church. This modest little man spoke these words to me that evening which I shall never forget: "When I started out, I wanted to find a place where I did not need to compete.

48

I found it on the Labrador coast. And I thank God that these old rough hands of mine, which have handled a ship's wheel more than they have wielded a surgeon's knife, have nevertheless, under God, been able to make blind men see and lame men walk."

No doubt there is someone in your life whom you have known well and in whose face you have "seen the eternal." Maybe not a famous person but a neighbor, a man or woman, unknown to the world but from whose presence you have come saying, "Surely I have seen God in this person."

CHAPTER FOUR

MAN CAN WIN THE BATTLE WITH EVIL

WE HAVE ALL LIVED IN THIS WORLD OF WONDER AND beauty long enough to know that alongside the good there is also much evil. If any of us has any doubt about this, let him take a look in several directions. On the table beside me as I eat my breakfast is the morning newspaper. In it I read that a man swindled the government out of some millions of dollars, a jealous husband killed his wife, a mother killed her four children because she said God told her to do it, a transport airliner fell and ninety-nine persons were killed, and a senator started a fist fight with another senator. Ambition, deception, immorality, and tragedy are all around us.

Then, lest we become self-righteous and imagine that all the evil in the world goes on outside us, let us take a look at ourselves. We don't murder, rob banks, or deliberately run down pedestrians with our automobiles. We don't do anything that marks us as violators of law and order. But we talk, and frequently the talk is vicious. We make statements which cannot be backed up by fact. We don't deliberately lie; we just do not tell the whole truth. We may not even talk. We can do a lot of harm in the world by a look or a gesture. We don't always do things that are positively wrong; we just don't do things that are good. We are negative characters.

Evil is real

It is hardly necessary to go into detail as to the origin of the evil we find around us and in us. I am sure that if anyone wishes to pursue the subject, he can find it in any number of books. He will discover, too, that different people have different explanations, but when it comes to the plain fact or evil, it is hard to believe that a man could be found anywhere who would deny it. Some people say that evil is only the absence of good, just as they say darkness is only the absence of light. But statements of this sort do not obscure the fact of the reality of evil or the fact that this night may be the blackest night ever.

My church in Chicago was located just a block off Madison Street, a street which social workers say is one of the worst streets in the world—if not the worst. All one had to do to find out how great the evils were was to walk a few blocks along the street. Derelicts of all sorts trooped into my study daily. They not only were warped physically, mentally, morally, and spiritually, but they were crushed by the steam roller of disease, sin, and destiny.

But evil is no respecter of persons, and it doesn't stop on Madison Street. It visits the boulevards, the palatial residences, and the better housing districts. We have watched evil do its harm in slums, in mansions, and on the farms. In any event, we can't think very far in religion until we come to some terms about the fact of evil in the world. Personally, I wish I didn't have to think about it at all, and no doubt most people wish they could get rid of evil; but the fact is that it is here and it is bound to stay with us as long as we live, and unless we think about it we won't know how to deal with it.

The evil outside us

I was a lad of six years when a huge flood swept through our village in central Pennsylvania. I was just old enough to remember a few details. The water swept through our property and destroyed my mother's beautiful garden; it took the pig pen and the chicken house and landed them a mile from home and marooned my father's horse in the barn for three days without food and water. Similar things were happening all through the village and around the countryside. Much property damage was done, and a few lives were lost. In later years I've seen block after block of houses in a city destroyed by fire, and I've seen epidemics of disease strike down hundreds of people.

When these things come, we call them natural evils—evils for which we are not responsible. We have asked ourselves a thousand times, Why did they happen? Why did God allow them to happen? Why do some people have to suffer so much, while others suffer so little? Obviously there is no way of getting an answer. God must allow them to happen else they would not be here, but that is about all we *do* know. We can't answer the question, Why?

We may blame the citizens of a community for their lethargy, their lack of foresight, or whatever one may call it, for not making provision to prevent the calamity. But are most of us any different? We lock the door only after the horse has been stolen. When calamity comes, people say, "This must not happen again." And frequently it doesn't happen again. Something good comes out of the calamity. Dayton, Ohio, had a devastating flood in 1913. The damage done and the loss of lives is almost beyond description. However, by the time I went there in 1917, the construction of dams along the Miami River had begun, and ever since that time Dayton could build as it wished without any fear of devastating floods. Some folk complained about the taxes necessary to pay the expense, but as is usually the case, what some thought to be a hardship was found to be a blessing to future generations.

I don't think a Christian can have any cut-and-dried answer as to why devastating evils such as flood, fire, and storm are visited upon people. He ought, however, to have something better to say, something which enables him to meet them in a triumphant manner if they *do* come. He does not presume to understand them. He does not know whence they come or why. But he does feel that no matter what may be visited upon him, God has not taken his hand off the steering wheel of the universe.

Maybe, too, we will come to know that God intended man to do certain things himself. For example, any number of lives have been saved by penicillin. Some few years ago we did not have that drug, and many people died because there was no way to kill the deadly germs. God in his infinite kindness must have been hoping ever since the morning stars sang together that some scientist would discover the law which would release penicillin. God doesn't go out to some high hill, wave a wand over the world, and perform miracles. He makes the laws of the universe eventually to break through to the mind of man. In the meantime a good man waits, does not become impatient, does not complain against God or become bitter. He handles things as well as he can and prays that somehow God will open his mind or the mind of another person to the wonders of God's power expressed through the laws of the universe.

If we are troubled about the presence of these natural evils in the world and would like a reason for them, let us go to the New Testament and see what Jesus said about them. But do not be surprised when you discover that Jesus made no explanation of evil. People then thought, as many do today, that evils are a punishment for a man's sin. But Jesus could not accept that. For example, Pilate had ordered the massacre of a group of Galileans while they were in the act of making their sacrifice to God. Did this happen, the people asked Jesus, because the Galileans were wicked and sinful? He answered, "I tell you, No; but unless you repent you will all likewise perish." Jesus didn't waste his time trying to explain evil. He set about to overcome the power of evil with the power of repentance.

The evil inside us

When we come to moral evil, we are on familiar ground, for the obvious reason that moral evil starts with you and me. What marvelous achievements have been wrought by the mind of man! When I was a boy, my father showed me pictures of airplanes made by Leonardo da Vinci and said to me, "Someday we'll fly. If a bird can fly, why can't a man? All we need is to know the law." But look what has been done with the airplane! Orville Wright said one night at a banquet in Dayton, Ohio, that if he and his brother Wilbur had known that what they were making would be used for wiping out whole cities, they might not have gone on with their invention. They never dreamed that it would be used for other than commercial purposes.

Look what happened to the freedom-loving spirit which made our forefathers break their old familiar moorings and come to these shores. These same people soon became tyrants, and men were put in stocks and some killed when they sought to exercise their God-given freedom to worship God according to the dictates of their conscience. Even in our day religionists have thought it necessary to engage in their own private persecution of those who did not conform to established religious practices.

It seems strange how man insists on spoiling so many good things which are put into his hands. The best thing that God ever bestowed upon man is love. Henry Drummond called it *The Greatest Thing in the World*. It is the thing that binds fathers and mothers to their children and the children to their parents and to one another. There isn't anything more wonderful than to see families enjoying themselves together and uniting their gaiety and work in one common enterprise for the family. Yet, right now in the world there is nothing that seems to be causing so much frustration and unhappiness as the family. What is and what ought to remain a blessing is turned into a curse by one or more members of the family whose minds are set in evil directions. We can count the number of divorces which occur in the course of a year, but there is no way of compiling statistics as to the number of unhappy families there are. I'm afraid if we knew we would be startled.

Moral evil gets into business too. The small businessman in any community can tell you of many unfair practices with which he must contend. I asked our groceryman about it, and he said, "You don't know the half of it. It is a wretched competitive game, and we small fellows have a hard time being honest. But I told my wife the other day that if I had to lie and cheat in order to make a living, I'd get out of the grocery business."

One would suppose that the one place there would be no evil is the church. But not so. In less than two centuries after Jesus walked the earth with a few disciples and taught the principles of the kingdom of God, the church was full of quarreling groups, superstition, and formality that killed the real essence of religion. I do not need to recount the many evils in the church which have made it a laughing-stock on so many occasions down through these two thousand years. The reason, of course, is that the church is made up not of angels but of imperfect human beings, and so long as this remains true, it will not be free from evils. Men can be as bad in church as in any other place in life.

So we come to the conclusion that good things can be spoiled—spoiled by us who are not as good as we could be. Why we are this way and why generations insist on repeating the evils of preceding generations is difficult to know. About the only conclusion we can come to is that regardless of its origin there is something evil in us.

A few years ago I inquired about a certain family who lived in our village when I was a lad. My informant said, "Oh, one boy became a suicide, a second one spent years in jail, and a third one was hanged for murder. You know, their parents were rather good people and respectable citizens, but the boys had a bad streak in them." No doubt they had, and there is something of a "bad streak" in all of us. I do not mean to imply that we are all horse thieves, bandits, or murderers. We've noted in another chapter that the world for the most part is made up of pretty good people, else there would be no place of safety for anyone. But somehow we are selfish, and we have a strong disposition to get what we want regardless of how much it may hurt other people. There are times when we do noble deeds and times we do ignoble deeds. At one time we will put ourselves out to do a kindness and to see that our neighbor gets a square deal; the next moment we act as though something were being filched from us, and we stand up for our own rights.

It is precisely at this point that hope for peace in the world can go on the rocks. It is this kind of selfish disposition that ruins families, individuals, churches, and even governments. I have often wished that we would occasionally stand up and tell the world that there is a bad streak in us, and we are sorry for it and will try to overcome it. We have done enough face-saving, so why not try to be downright honest with others and with ourselves and acknowledge that we can and do make mistakes. The only time anyone can do anything about achieving a more perfect character is when he brings his sins out into the sunlight and sees them for what they are. The amazing thing is how faultfinding we can be about other people's evils and how blissfully unaware we are of our own.

How shall we overcome evil?

The religion of Jesus has positive help to give us. It has not been content to settle for a permanent "bad streak" in us or even in our first parents, Adam and Eve. I do not argue any doctrine of original sin, for if it is true that we were born with some sin in us, it is also true that most of us were born with a lot of good in us too! Even in the Adam and Eve story in Genesis it is reported that when God looked at his creation, he "saw every thing that he had made, and behold, it was very good." I remember an occasion at a college convocation when I heard a fellow speaker say to a thousand boys and girls that he knew for a fact that God created men to his own glory and damned them to his own glory. My hair stood on end! I could not then nor can I now associate myself with such an utterly pagan idea of God. I don't believe that God, who made a creation and called it good, would secretly also make it evil.

I watched a contractor build a road past my house. He built a good road, and you can rest assured that when he mixed the asphalt, he didn't put something into it to make it deteriorate. To be sure, it will deteriorate in time as heavy trucks pound at it and cold winter nights put frosts into it—but our contractor didn't create the road with those evils in it. By the same kind of reasoning I reject the notion of some theologians that God made man with some inner deteriorating forces; I believe that he made man well and that he endowed him with basic goodness.

To add to the possibility of man's strength, God endowed man with the power of choice. Man can choose good, and he can choose evil. I believe that because of that freedom we exercise, there are evil things within us because we made evil choices and there are good things in us because we have made good choices. We can love, or we can hate. We can live in the upper regions of God's universe, or we can sink into the cesspools about us. Like one driving an automobile, we can drive it carefully and according to the law—or we can disregard the laws and be reckless. In the first instance we can enjoy safety and experience satisfaction; in the second instance we can endanger our lives as well as the lives of others.

It is not a contradiction in terms to say that strength is humble. For the Christian this is not a strange use of the word. If we have reached the place where our all-sufficient, proud-of-ourselves attitude has become uppermost, then we are in a most dangerous position. Christianity's use of the word "humility" is good common sense, not some expression of milk and water virtue; it is the mainspring of all virtues. Humility that is genuine—and there isn't any other kind—enables man to roll with the punches. Man's triumphs and defeats cannot be met without the grace of humility, for the proud fall and the defeated never get to their feet. The adage "Those whom the gods would destroy they first make mad" is proved over and over again when man is possessed by his possessions, and the symptoms of the madness are selfishness, bigotry, and narrow-mindedness. Humility makes it possible for the real man to overcome evil with good.

The religion of Jesus does not stop at the point of making a man strong within himself, however, for it recognizes that "none of us liveth to himself." Man soon learns that a defense against the world of people is a pretty lonely way of life, and to bridge the gap between himself and his fellow men, he discovers that he must participate successfully in the affairs of the human race. Read between the lines in that story of the prodigal son sometime and see the principle of isolationism in the attitude of the elder brother. He has been overlooked by many of us as we have easily condemned the younger brother! You get the feeling that the elder brother was almost glad that the prodigal had taken leave of the farm, and certainly it was clear that he didn't want to see him come home for "he was angry, and would not go in" when the old father welcomed the sinner home. I don't know how it ever worked out, but the elder brother was a tragic figure for the rest of his life if his childish jealousy kept him forever from "going in." I know people like that, and most of us have had similar moments in our lives when we have stood outside pouting like spoiled children —but I also know that I must "go in" if I am to "snap out of it" and become a happy and functioning person.

Of equal importance in any successful relationship with community is the Christian's attitude concerning less fortunate human beings. There was a time when we thought of this as a kind of vague benevolent feeling, like the rich people being sorry for the poor people. We gave our old worn-out clothes to the heathen Africans (who didn't want them or wear them) , or we tossed a bit of food to the starving people in some far-off place and satisfied ourselves that we were being very nice and very Christian. But this was not doing anything for anybody! We have learned that the struggle to be is abroad in the world and that the "have-nots" will not go on forever being satisfied with not having. The shift from the old benevolent idea to "helping people help themselves" is taking place. The Christian cannot depend on isolation from the unfortunate anymore than he can successfully isolate himself from the fortunate. His being fortunate or unfortunate is bound up tightly with the welfare of all mankind everywhere.

Is it necessary to mention prayer? Surely if one is to confess sins, seek guidance in his choices, develop the grace of humility, and live well with his fellow men, he must be in communication with the Source of all. Prayer is man's reach for God and God's reach for man. It is a way of life, not an occasional exercise. It is the climax and all-inclusive process that keeps man at his best.

CHAPTER FIVE

JESUS BELIEVED IN MAN

IF THERE HAD BEEN A *Who's Who* IN THE DAYS OF JESUS, a short biographical sketch of him might have read after this fashion: Born in Bethlehem in the year 4 B.C.; parents, Joseph and Mary; reared in Nazareth, a city of no account; a bachelor; occupation, carpenter; not educated in the schools and colleges; short public career of about eighteen months at most; tried and convicted of treason against the state and put to death on a cross; he was translated to heaven.

If this were the time and place to write about the details of that life, I should be happy to do so. However, let me just say one or two things which seem to fit into what we shall have to say about Jesus' belief in man. He had a Godlike desire to love all kinds of men and women. One of the charges his accusers made against him was that he was a friend of publicans and sinners, a gluttonous man and a winebibber. Wherever he went, he brought a radiance that people could see and feel. He made bad men want to be good and small men, to be great. Although he often saw life lived on its lowest level, nevertheless his actions were always such that men could see that he loved them. He preached a little, but he ministered more; and when he died and was laid in a tomb, people couldn't think of him as remaining there. He had made of the earth while he was here as much of a heaven as he could make it, and it was in heaven that he belonged at his death. He identified himself with the lowliest of men, and they put him at the top of life, where he has remained ever since.

A student once took a photograph of a mountain pass in Switzerland. When this was developed, there appeared in it, part of the way up the long, sinuous mountain trail, the solitary figure of a man, all but lost among the peaks. The photograph, which was to have shown the majesty of the mountains, became far more significant because of the man struggling up the slippery crag. It was an artist's and a philosopher's instinct that took the picture just at that moment. The figure of the man throws new light on nature.

This illustrates the way the mind of Jesus worked. There is nothing in the Gospels to indicate that Jesus was deeply moved by art or architecture. He must have loved nature else he never would have said, "Consider the lilies how they grow," and he never would have talked about birds or flowers or vineyards. But all the lessons he drew from nature were directed toward the development of human personality.

His one main interest was people. He was solicitous about their food and clothing, sensitive to their hunger, and his heart went out to the maimed, the sick, the blind, the sinful. He was touched by the sight of all unhappy folk. One can read account after account of his tenderness and care in the presence of misery and helplessness.

When the author of the Fourth Gospel wrote the prologue and talked about the Light that had come into the world, he said that the "life was the Light for men: amid the darkness the Light shone, but the darkness did not master it." If we could keep this thought uppermost in our minds, we would have little to despair of, no matter how wicked we think the world and individuals are, for Jesus was bearing about with him a light that no darkness could put out, and it will keep on shining in the hearts of men.

Jesus cared deeply about sinners

There are a number of incidents in the New Testament which depict the manner in which Jesus dealt with individuals, but one stands out in compassion, in love, and in tenderness above all others. It is the incident which occurred in the home of Simon the Pharisee when the woman came to anoint the feet of Jesus. Not only does it reveal Jesus' method of love but also the wholesome respect which he had for the individual—any individual, regardless of the place or position in life which he occupied. Jesus felt compelled to turn any sufferer's face toward some patch of blue where all before had seemed gray.

I am sure it would be to our everlasting good if we would turn our eyes upon that scene, for the simple reason that in our human relationships we are bound to come upon both Simon and the woman. They live in our town and walk our streets, and if we go to church we see them there.

Jesus is at the house of a wealthy Pharisee and no doubt reclining comfortably at a well-laden table.

Now there was a woman in the town who was a sinner, and when she found out that Jesus was at table in the house of the Pharisee, she brought an alabaster flask of perfume and stood behind him at his feet in tears; as her tears began to wet his feet, she wiped them with the hair of her head, pressed kisses on them, and anointed them with perfume.

Where the woman had seen Jesus before, we do not know. It may be that sometime she had stood at the edge of a crowd and listened to him. Maybe someone had told her about him. At any rate, she knew him. The dining room opened out on the street after the Oriental custom of building houses, and the woman could see him as she passed. She heard his voice, and it must have been one of compassion. Asking no questions and waiting for no invitation but with deep longing in her heart for a changed life, she walked in, knelt at his feet, and poured out her soul in the only way she knew.

It must have been a strange sight to Simon the Pharisee. No such person had ever been in his house before. He was aghast, and all he could splutter was, "She is a sinner." She was an untouchable, and if Jesus were a prophet as he claimed to be, he could recognize her as such. Even the guests were amazed. But Jesus was not startled at all. There was nothing unusual about it. Others had come kneeling before him, and still others would crave his blessing down to the last day of his life.

But Jesus put a staying hand on Simon as Simon attempted to put her out and told him this story:

"There was a moneylender who had two debtors; one owed him fifty pounds, the other five. As they were unable to pay, he freely forgave them both. Tell me, now, which of them will love him most?" "I suppose," said Simon, "the man who had most forgiven." "Quite right," [Jesus] said. Then turning to the woman he said to Simon, "You see this woman? When I came into your house, you never gave me water for my feet, while she has wet my feet with her tears and wiped them with her hair; you never gave me a kiss, while ever since she came in she has kept pressing kisses on my feet; you never anointed my head with oil, while she has anointed my feet with perfume. Therefore I tell you, many as her sins are, they are forgiven, for her love is great; whereas he to whom little is forgiven has but little love." And he said to her, "Your sins are forgiven. . . . Your faith has saved you; go in peace."

If we want proof that Jesus never despaired of any individual, we should not miss this story. It happened two thousand years ago, but we still have Simon the Pharisee, and we still have the woman and her class. We still have the "healing of His seamless dress," and we know when folk "touch Him in life's throng and press" that they are "whole again." It is a moving incident and the parable of the two debtors which lies at its center has not lacked for comment. But it is not the parable which concerns us here. We are thinking of the attitudes we show toward individuals—not those whom we know, not those who sit at our tables and are well dressed and who know the details of social etiquette. The question is, How do we deal with wrongdoers? There is the way of Simon—"She is a sinner." There is the way still other people deal with the sinner. They find it hard to believe that a leopard can change its spots. There is at last Jesus' way—the right way. It would make a difference in a church, in a community, if we would sit down before this conversation between Simon and Jesus and mark the contrast between how Jesus looks at the individual and how the individual is regarded by other people, including ourselves.

We can choose Simon's way if we wish. Many do. All he could say was, "She is a sinner." And he was right. She was.

Any parent would tremble for a daughter if she were to make friends with such a woman. Even a kind and merciful Son of God can find no assuring words to say of her sin. "Her sins are many," he said. But is that all we have to say? To denounce such a one as a sinner and leave it at that does not fill up the measure of the Christian ethic. The spirit of contempt had no place in the life of Jesus. And it has no place in the life of any who would be Christlike.

Jesus knew men could be redeemed

If the woman was to be redeemed and set in the rightful place from which she had fallen, it couldn't be done by means of Simon's contempt and scorn. People are not saved by that process—neither lustful folk such as the woman nor greedy and selfish folk such as Simon. Satan does not cast out Satan. Men such as Simon might gorge themselves with food and drink copiously, but Jesus would not condemn them. He ate with Simon and was generous toward him as toward the woman. We know nothing about the future of Simon, but if his spirit of contempt and scorn was finally changed to love and sympathy, it would have been caused by the firm but kind attitude of Jesus in his house that day.

Perhaps the woman in Simon's house had been hearing the doctrine of fatalism preached. When she told her story to her neighbors and expressed the wish to be different, they laughed at her and told her she could do nothing about the kind of life she had been living. She was chained to a lustful existence, and there she would have to remain.

So certain men speak today. Conduct cannot be changed, they say. We have certain inclinations; we've been set going in certain directions and are driven relentlessly without any hope of changing. Psychology has done much to show the baneful effects of "complexes." But complexes are not the final determinant in life. They do not decide the issue. It is possible for anyone in the position of the woman to look steadily at the thing that is hurting and realize that in the end it has no real power to injure if it is honestly faced.

We must never forget how Jesus looked at the woman. He knew the difference between right and wrong. He was sensitive to the evil in men's lives. He prayed for Peter. He worked patiently with all the disciples in the hope that someday they would find the good triumphing over the evil in their lives. He knew the difference between goats and sheep. Harsh, selfish, cruel men would have to take their place with the goats in the day of judgment. Those who gave food to the hungry, drink to the thirsty, clothing to the naked, visited the sick and those in prison, would stand with the sheep in judgment. Jesus would never have put this woman in the class with his mother. He believed there was a tremendous difference between the woman who kept her honor even at the cost of a long, hard struggle and the woman who sold herself as cheap merchandise. He kept his moral distinctions clear.

But there was something in him which went beyond sensitiveness to evil. He had an eye for what a person might become. When he chose disciples, he saw what they could be. He saw beneath the exterior. He knew that an occasional outburst of animal nature does not make a man a beast. He saw the womanly in the woman. He saw his opportunity, not to condemn her but to raise her to the place in which she belonged.

He let Simon know that people of the woman's sort are not to be treated as dirt under men's feet, that people are not in the world to be kicked into the street. They are God's children and must be given a chance. The final test of religion is not a man's prayers or sacrifices or position, but how he treats his neighbor. Life isn't things. It is quality of mind and heart. The moral life of man is not something which can be isolated from his personality as a whole. Redemption is the deliverance of personality from all the evil that has invaded and ravaged it.

This is what Jesus believed as he walked about and sat by the seaside and in the homes of people. This is the Good News, not good advice, which has come down to individual men everywhere. Most of us have failed miserably. We don't know what life is. To some of us it is greed; to some, money; to others, social connections; while to still others, a nominal connection with the church. It is none of these. "This is life eternal, that they might know thee the only true God, and Jesus Christ, whom thou hast sent."

We are alike, yet unalike

But Jesus did not see only the individual person. His interest was not in any special individual or class but in people as a whole. His interest in average people was a distinct contribution he made to the world. It was this attitude which got him into trouble with the authorities.

Jesus must, however, have found it difficult to believe in some men. One can hardly conceive of his being a carpenter, engaging in an occupation where he had to deal with all sorts of people, without coming into contact with some people who were not easy to like and trust. There were some who cheated, some who would not pay, some who beat him down in price, and some who were dissatisfied without cause with his workmanship. When he laid down his carpenter tools to engage in the business of being an itinerant preacher and teacher, he found the same kind of men.

Indeed, he found some who were worse than he had seen in the carpenter shop in Nazareth. He found men who thanked God that they were not as other men. He found some who thought more of money than of people in distress. There was Dives, the rich man, who was clothed in purple and fine linen and who fared sumptuously every day, while Lazarus, the beggar at his door, asked only to live on the crumbs that fell from the table. Moreover, he learned that there were people in his own country who could put such a noble man as John the Baptist to death. It was this knowledge that sent him out to pray in a desert place, where he could regain his belief in man and where he could have his sensitiveness to the cry of the crowd restored.

He would go away and regain his poise. But the people followed him on foot out of the cities. Tramp, tramp, came thousands of feet as the crowd moved up the hill in his direction. Had we been in his position, we might have become peevish, even snarled: "Can I never get away from this waiting and demanding multitude?" But Jesus belonged to them. They were his people. He was the one bright spot in all their drab and weary lives. He was different from their teachers. Life flowed through his veins, and a new religious vista was opened before the gaze of the multitude.

One of the things we should all be afraid of is becoming blind to the needs of the crowd. If I am a statesman, I must hear the cry of my constituency for just and righteous dealings. If I am an engineer, I must not throw a bridge across a river just to show my skill. If I am a doctor, I must not prevent or cure a disease merely to show my ability. If I am a preacher, I must not live in the clouds but walk the hot, steaming earth where men toil and sweat. I do not know how far Jesus proceeded with any formal education—perhaps further than the scant record indicates. But however great his knowledge of ideas, facts, and theories, he never forgot the language of the human heart. His eyes were always toward humanity, and not a day passed that he did not think of how he could break the bread of happiness to the multitude.

There are some things which you and I will see mirrored in the people around us if we look long enough. We expect to see something utterly different in other people. But this is not so. Rather, we are like the two frogs who lived in neighboring towns. One day they started out, each heading toward the other, both intent upon seeing what sort of land lay behind the hill that separated their homelands. They met at the summit, and each stood erect for a quick preview of the other's place. Naturally, with their eyes on the tops of their heads, like respectable frogs everywhere, each frog's gaze turned backward along the route he had taken. So, with a certain amount of grumbling and complaint they decided to return to their homes. "For," as one said to the other, "everything in your country is exactly as it is in mine."

How are we alike—you and me and the crowd we see around us? It is true that some have more money, some have a better place to live, some have had greater opportunities, some have more brains. But when it is all summed up, aside from the accidents of birth and the material existence of life, a man is still a man. The universe is as friendly to one as to another. The same sun shines on the rich and the poor, and God sends his rain upon the just and the unjust. Joy and sorrow, sickness and health, are no respecters of persons. Money can buy things, but it can't buy the peace that passeth understanding. Intellectual achievement may produce satisfaction, but it can't heal a broken heart or produce a contrite spirit. One man comes to the same end as another. At the last every man goes to his own place.

In the same mirror, in the same crowd, a man sees what he ought to be. Along with the feeling that we are one with humanity, there comes the knowledge of how different we are. There is no other person just like you or me. We are separate personalities. When we realize this, we can begin to take stock of our endowments. Maybe we have fine minds. We can reason when others become confused. Maybe we possess a fine personality. Each of us has many gifts, any one of which may be used to give our families a living, to provide us with the comforts of life. But all other people in the world present an opportunity to us. If a divine spark has been set on fire in the altar of our hearts, we can begin to say, "All these gifts I owe to the peoples of the world." We are fired with a noble impulse, and we ask, "Where can I take hold? To what human cause can I dedicate my gifts?"

This does not imply pity. Jesus never pitied men. Pity always carries with it a certain contempt. When he found the impotent man waiting for the pool at Bethesda to be troubled, he took him by the hand and told him to go home. To the man with the withered hand he said, "Stretch forth your hand." It is doubtful if any man wants pity. We sometimes imagine that Jesus pitied the poor because he was poor. But if we reason better, we will understand that his kindness had deeper roots—it was because of his respect for all the creatures of God. He never set up class distinctions. Even his accusers felt the force of his tenderness.

Jesus taught men two great qualities in relation to the problem of the crowd: to find themselves and to be of service to humanity without becoming lost in the crowd. This he demonstrated when he spoke to the doctors and lawyers in the Temple, when he saw the merchants and soldiers by the River Jordan, and when he came down from the mountain and met a troubled father pleading for healing for his paralytic son. Certainly he was a nature lover. He breathed in the perfume of flowers, rejoiced in the growing grain, responded to the songs of birds, and was captivated with the heights of the mountain peaks. But these were not enough. What he died for was not a bird or a flower, or a grain of wheat, but the multitudes of people. Always it was the low murmur of the crowd, the eager faces, the pictures of suffering and joy, that crowded in upon him by day and by night.

Jesus believes in every individual

Jesus never lost the individual in the crowd. Each person was a distinct personality. When the crowd on one occasion pressed upon him, he knew that it was a person in distress who touched his garment. With a sea of faces before him he sensed the need of one man, Zacchaeus, in the sycamore tree. And when the crowd kept pressing up the hillside, he saw the hunger of this child, the distress of this widow, the economic pressure upon this man.

To Jesus there was no such thing as the individual on the one hand and the crowd on the other. Seeing Jesus surrounded with people who had the same hopes, longings, and aspirations as have people of today, I think he would tell us if he were here right now that individual freedom comes only when society is perfected, and when the individual knows the true meaning of freedom, he will make his perfect contribution to society. Sin, repentance, and a new spirit must get hold of both society and the individual. We'll never get anywhere in any period of the world's history by frantic assertions of rugged individualism on the one hand and elaborate plans for the building of the social structure on the other hand. If the golden age of peace is to come and if nations are to live at peace with one another, it will be through man's patient and unselfish doing his best for the good of all. The person, the group, that makes the greatest contribution to joyful and complete living is one who loses neither the multitude in the man nor the man in the multitude.

Carlyle once led Emerson through the worst streets of London at midnight, then asked: "Do you believe in the devil now?" Emerson replied that the more he saw of the English people the better he thought of them. But Sir Henry Jones, who tells the story, commented: "Emerson's victory was not won in the enemy's citadel where sin sits throned amidst the chaos, but in the placid upper air of poetic imagination."

It was not so with Jesus. He won his victory in the citadel where sin and suffering sat enthroned amidst the chaos. He knew the sin of mankind, but he believed in man so much that he was willing to die for him.

NOTES